CLAVERDON PRIMARY SCHOOL
BREACH LANE
CLAVERDON
WARWICK
CV35 8QA

SCIENCE IN OUR WORLD

REPRODUCTION
and
HEREDITY

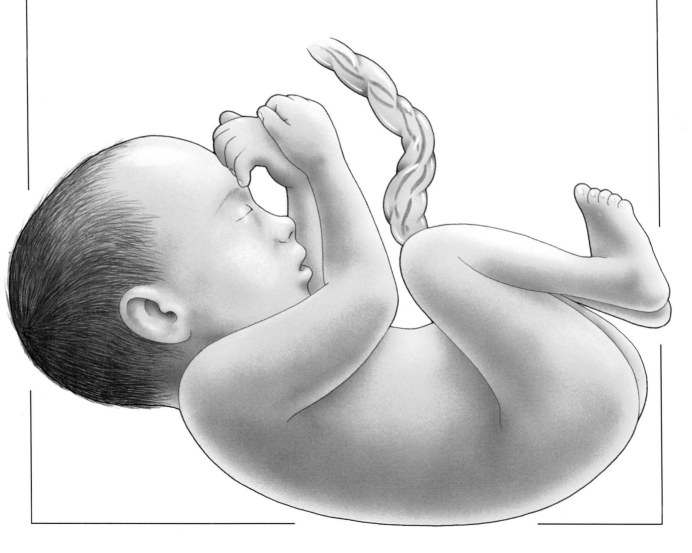

Contributory Author
Brian Knapp, BSc, PhD
Art Director
Duncan McCrae, BSc
Special Illustrations
David Woodroffe
Editorial consultant
Rita Owen, BSc and Sarah George, BEd
Special photography
Ian Gledhill
Science advisor
Martin Morris, BA, BEd
Print consultants
Landmark Production Consultants Ltd.
Printed and bound in Hong Kong
Produced by
EARTHSCAPE EDITIONS

First published in the United Kingdom in 1993
by Atlantic Europe Publishing Company Limited,
86 Peppard Road, Sonning Common, Reading,
Berkshire, RG4 9RP UK
Telephone 0734 723751; Fax 0734 724488

Publication Data
Knapp, Brian
    Reproduction and Heredity – (Science in our world; 24)
    1. Reproduction – For children
    2. Heredity – For children
    I. Title   II. Series
575.1
            ISBN 1-869860-97-7

In this book you will find some words that have been shown in **bold** type. There is a full explanation of each of these words on pages 46 and 47.

Experiments that you might like to try for yourself have been put in a yellow box like this.

Acknowledgements
The publishers would like to thank the following:
Dr. Angus McCrae, Charles Schotman and
Leighton Park School.

Picture credits
t=top b=bottom l=left r=right
All illustrations are from the Earthscape Editions library.
Dr. Savile Bradbury was responsible for taking the
following pictures: 2bl, 11tr, 11r, 11bl, 12tr, 14l, 26/27, 26l.

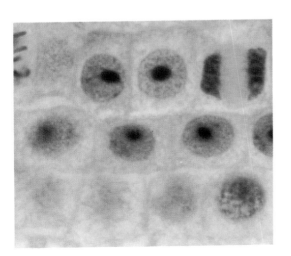

Contents

Introduction

fossils
page 42

hybrids
page 34

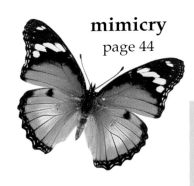

mimicry
page 44

viruses
page 30

cereals
page 36

natural selection
page 40

Look into the faces of your parents, brothers and sisters: do you notice any similarities? These resemblances are not accidental; they are there because you and your brothers and sisters have **inherited** these characteristics from either one or both of your parents. This is known as heredity.

It is not only people who inherit from their parents. All living things share some characteristics with each parent who in turn share some of their characteristics with their parents and so on.

Many of the plants in your home or at school will have been specially bred by gardeners to show off certain characteristics, such as large flowers, or brightly-coloured leaves. In the same way domestic animals, such as cats and dogs, are bred for certain characteristics, for example fluffy coats, long ears or a

green genes
page 38

genes
page 10

embryo
page 24

4

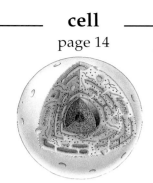

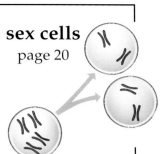

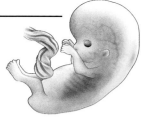

particular colour pattern. This is why there is such a variety of cat and dog breeds.

However, it is never certain that every offspring will inherit all the desired characteristics. For example, people who breed racehorses can never be sure that the foals that are born to winning horses will themselves turn out to be great racehorses.

Scientists now understand many of the processes that control the way characteristics, such as colour, are passed on. We now know how a single **fertilised egg** can become a complete person after just nine months. Scientists are also beginning to understand how certain inherited illnesses are caused and even how to put them right.

Find out about **reproduction** and heredity in any way you choose. Just turn to a page to begin your discoveries.

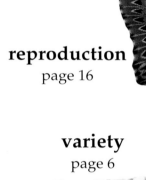

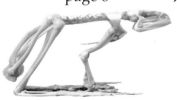

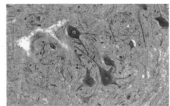

The variety of life

No-one knows for sure how many different **species** inhabit our world, but it is probably over three million.

Humans make up just one species and are part of a group of animals called **mammals**.

Many species have existed unchanged for a long time and the remains of their ancestors can be found as **fossils** in rocks thousands of millions of years old.

Reproduction is the way living things reproduce themselves; heredity is about the way each species passes on the information needed to make new life.

LIVING THINGS

THE PLANT KINGDOM

FUNGI

SINGLE-CELLED NO CELL MEMBRANE

NON-FLOWERING SIMPLE PLANTS
Examples are:
liverworts, mosses, lichens, ferns, algae

SEED-PRODUCING PLANTS
Examples are:
oak trees, grasses, pine trees, lilies, strawberries and potatoes

Examples are:
yeasts, mushrooms and toadstools

Examples are:
bacteria and blue-green algae

Lichen

Lily

The largest living thing is a conifer, the giant Redwood tree of western USA.

Oak

Mushroom

Bacteria have been found over 41,000 m above the Earth's surface

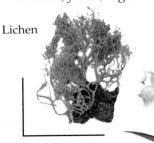

The flow chart below shows a simple classification of all living things.

The living world

The enormous variety of life on Earth can be classified in the way shown in the chart below. Animals and plants can be grouped by similarities in features and ancestry.

But what do we share with all other animals and plants when we are all so different? The answer was discovered by scientists only when they looked at the smallest fragments of life, hidden deep inside every **cell** of every live thing. It carries the coded information for life and is called a **gene**.

Reproduction is the means by which this information is passed on from generation to generation. All living things (except some cross-breeds) are capable of reproduction.

THE ANIMAL KINGDOM

ANIMALS WITH BACKBONES
Examples are:
fish, frogs, lizards, snakes, birds and mammals including human beings

The largest living animal in the world is a mammal, the Blue Whale, which has been recorded at over 30 m in length.

ANIMALS WITHOUT BACKBONES
Examples are:
snails, jellyfish, lobsters, centipedes, millipedes, earthworms, insects and sea urchins

There are more than 3 million animal species known.

SINGLE-CELLED WITH CELL MEMBRANE

Examples are:
malaria parasites, amoebae

Frog

Frog skeleton

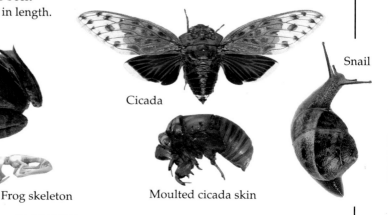
Cicada

Moulted cicada skin

Snail

Variety between generations

One of the most interesting ways of studying heredity is to look at your own family. If you can get them all together, or collect pictures of them, you will be able to arrange them into a pattern called a family tree. By comparing facial features alone, you will be able to see how **traits** are passed on and how change gradually occurs from one generation to the next.

Passing on traits

Sometimes we can see quite clearly that traits are passed on from parents to their children. From household photographs of family groups showing several generations you can see some very close similarities and yet also some differences in facial features, hair and eye colour, size and shape. Some features seem to be more persistent or dominant and appear more frequently within generations. Other traits appear in one generation and are missed out by the next only to appear again in the third. In some cases, such as hair colour, these features are controlled by a single gene. In most cases they are controlled by several genes.

(For more information on family trees see the book Time *in the Science in our world series.)*

Look for inherited traits

The pictures on these pages are all of large family groups. Try to spot the similar traits within each group.

Can you spot which members have married into the family group?

Mixing characteristics

Although it is possible for many species to reproduce without two parents (for example, greenfly, see page 16), and it is possible for people within the same family group to have children, this greatly increases the chances of passing on diseases by inheritance. Species become best adapted to survive by mixing characteristics from those who are not closely related.

Genes

The most basic information that instructs our body in the way it will develop is passed on from parents to offspring in chemical packages called genes. They are chemical messengers containing the information for making all other chemicals needed for life, especially for making **proteins**, which are the building blocks of all cells.

Genes are strung out on a large coiled **molecule** called **DNA**, rather like beads on a thread. Messages are constantly being sent from the genes on the DNA to tell the cell how to behave and what kind of cell to make. It is vital, therefore, that the DNA molecule with its genes occurs inside every cell.

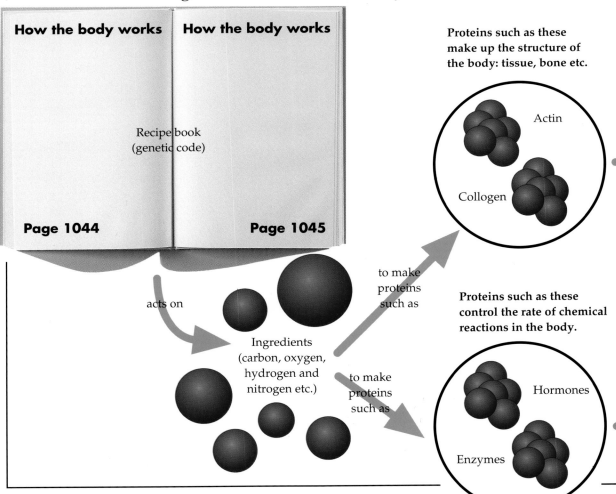

How the body works

How the body works

Recipe book
(genetic code)

Page 1044

Page 1045

acts on

Ingredients
(carbon, oxygen,
hydrogen and
nitrogen etc.)

to make
proteins
such as

to make
proteins
such as

Proteins such as these
make up the structure of
the body: tissue, bone etc.

Actin

Collogen

Proteins such as these
control the rate of chemical
reactions in the body.

Hormones

Enzymes

Genes and proteins

Perhaps the simplest way of describing how genes give instructions is to think of them as a recipe book which lays down rules for working with ingredients.

Suppose the ingredients are eggs, flour, butter and water. Made up one way they will make dumplings, made another way they will give pancakes, and made a third way they will give bread. The recipe as such (the genes) does nothing, it is the ingredients (the proteins) that fit together in special ways to make up the cells, but without the genes to instruct them, the proteins would not come together in the right way.

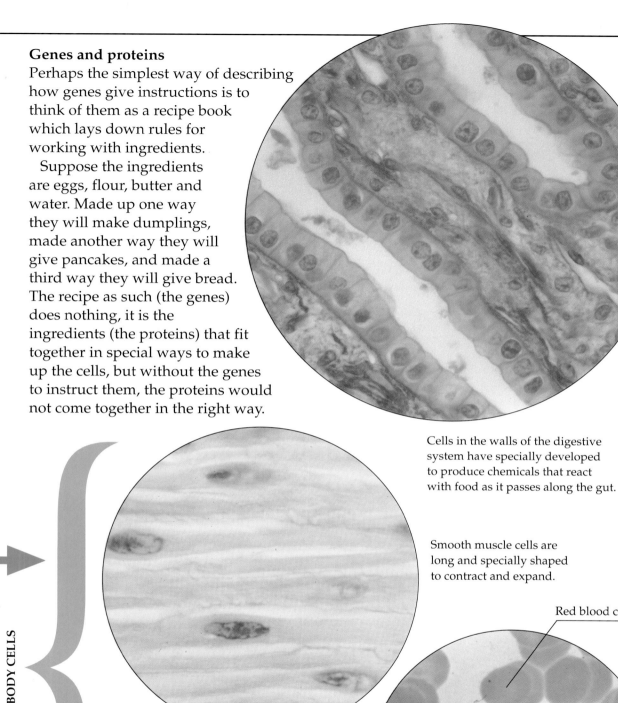

Cells in the walls of the digestive system have specially developed to produce chemicals that react with food as it passes along the gut.

Smooth muscle cells are long and specially shaped to contract and expand.

Red blood cells

BODY CELLS

Red blood cells carry oxygen to the tissues of the body. White blood cells try to attack any foreign bodies such as bacteria that enter the blood stream.

White blood cell

11

How genes are organised

There are more than fifty trillion cells in the human body and nearly all of them have their own genetic information. In every case the genes are organised along a long coiled molecule called DNA. This holds the secrets of heredity.

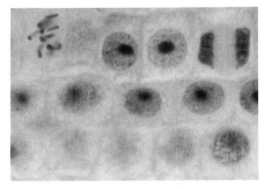

This picture shows what chromosomes look like inside cells. This view is magnified about 1000 times.

DNA: the heredity molecule

The string-like DNA molecule is so long that it has to be coiled tightly simply to fit into the central region, or nucleus, of a cell. Sometimes it forms thread-like structures that can be seen under an ordinary microscope and these are called chromosomes.

In the simplest organisms, such as bacteria and algae, all the DNA is found in a single chromosome. In more complex organisms there is too much information to be carried in a single chromosome. In humans, for example, there are 46 chromosomes in each cell.

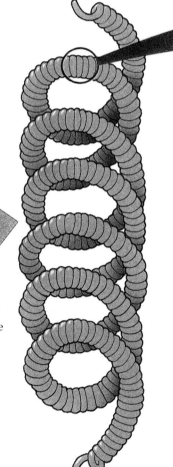

1 The most powerful microscopes are able to see inside the central region (nucleus) of a cell. Here long string-like bodies called chromosomes can be seen.

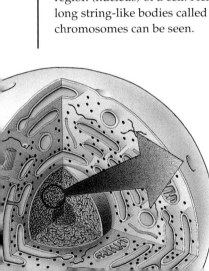

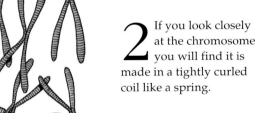

2 If you look closely at the chromosome you will find it is made in a tightly curled coil like a spring.

Genes

A gene is a specific piece of information in the form of a chemical instruction. This chemical instruction is part of the DNA molecule. Very large numbers of such genes are needed to provide the recipe for a living thing and they all have to be kept in a strict order.

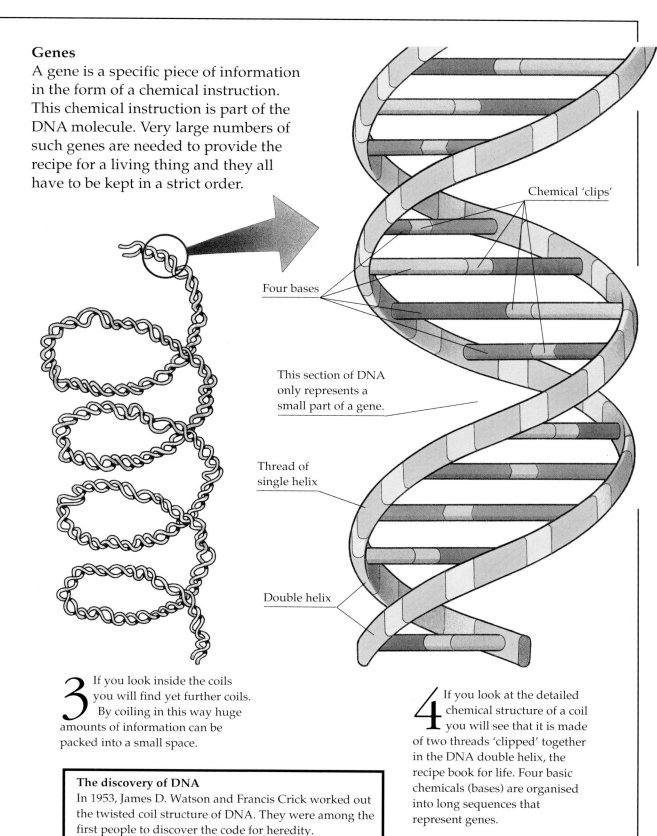

Chemical 'clips'

Four bases

This section of DNA only represents a small part of a gene.

Thread of single helix

Double helix

3 If you look inside the coils you will find yet further coils. By coiling in this way huge amounts of information can be packed into a small space.

4 If you look at the detailed chemical structure of a coil you will see that it is made of two threads 'clipped' together in the DNA double helix, the recipe book for life. Four basic chemicals (bases) are organised into long sequences that represent genes.

The discovery of DNA
In 1953, James D. Watson and Francis Crick worked out the twisted coil structure of DNA. They were among the first people to discover the code for heredity.

Inside the cell

All living things are made up of one or more cells. Each plant and animal cell has two regions – an outer shell (the membrane) whose purpose is to keep the cell alive and well, and an inner core (the nucleus) which is concerned with cell reproduction.

The genes and the DNA occur inside the nucleus and send out instructions controlling the development of the cell.

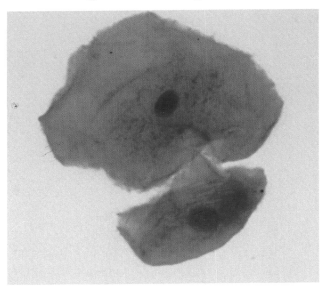

You can see some of the detail of cells through a normal microscope although they are always in the form of thin slices. The cells in the picture above are from inside the mouth and show the nucleus clearly.

Discovery of the cell
The word 'cell' was first used by the English Scientist Robert Hooke in 1665. When he looked at cork under a microscope he saw it was made of small closed compartments that reminded him of the cells found in monasteries and prisons.

Molecules for making cell material (such as protein) and providing energy are transported into the cell fluids through the porous membrane.

A chemical factory
You can think of a cell as a chemical factory. The cell absorbs nourishment through the membrane wall and uses this to make the energy needed for life's processes.

Waste products and other chemicals are transported out of the cell through the membrane.

Drawn to the same scale as the cell model (above right), the distance between these arrowheads represents one tenth of the width of a human hair.

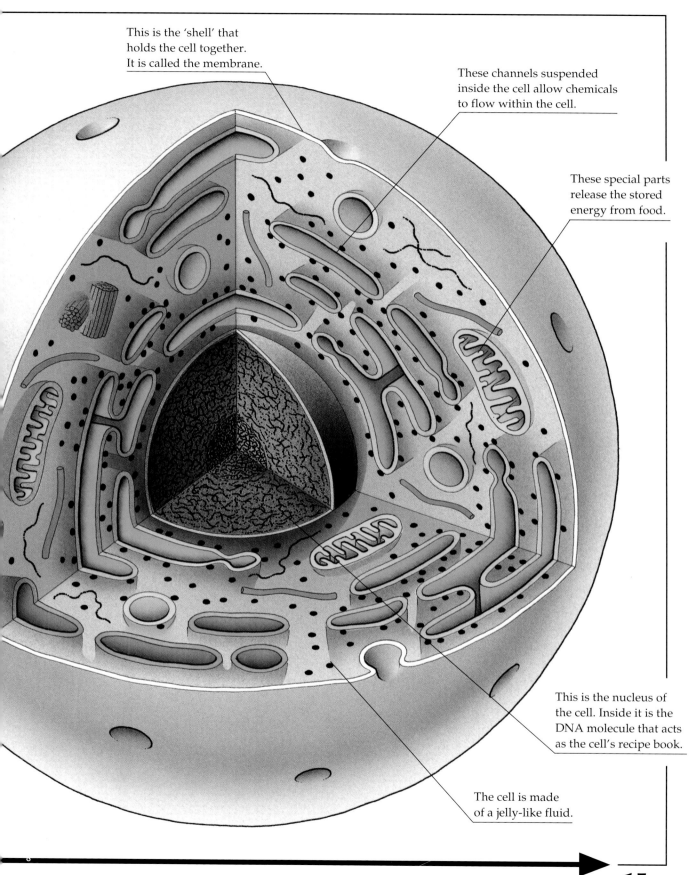

This is the 'shell' that holds the cell together. It is called the membrane.

These channels suspended inside the cell allow chemicals to flow within the cell.

These special parts release the stored energy from food.

This is the nucleus of the cell. Inside it is the DNA molecule that acts as the cell's recipe book.

The cell is made of a jelly-like fluid.

The two ways of reproducing

There are two ways of producing new life. One requires only a single parent (see page 18) and it is a fast way of making new copies. The other is slower and more complicated (see page 20), but it creates variety. This gives new life a better chance to adapt to changing environments.

Plants and animals take advantage of both forms of reproduction to give themselves the best chance of survival.

(see page 18)
(see page 20)

Famous scientists and heredity

The three scientists best remembered for their work on heredity are Jean Baptiste Lamarck, who lived in the eighteenth century, and Charles Darwin and Gregor Mendel, who both lived in the nineteenth century.

Lamarck believed that people changed because of their surroundings. For example, he believed that giraffes have long necks because their ancestors were always stretching their necks to get to the leaves high in the trees.

Darwin believed that there were naturally many variations within a species and that those variations which best adapted individuals to live in a particular environment (**niche**) would be more likely to survive and to have offspring. He called this Natural Selection (see page 41).

Gregor Mendel discovered how traits were passed from one generation to another from his experiments with breeding peas.

From these important ideas, modern scientists gradually realised that there has to be a '**blueprint**', or 'recipe book' for life contained in every cell.

(see page 41)

This parent spider plant has produced many copies of itself along stems.
Each plantlet can take root and live a separate life. This is one way this plant reproduces.

Copying

When a parent produces new life on its own, it is producing exact copies, or replicas. Most of the cells in our bodies are created this way (see page 18).

Copying is a very fast and efficient way of increasing numbers and many plants and insects use this system to great effect when colonising a new environment. For example, at the beginning of summer some plants send out 'runners' which then shoot at special points and produce miniature plants that can take root.

There are also many examples of insects that rapidly replicate themselves. A female greenfly, for example, can produce many copies of herself without the need for a male.

(see page 18)

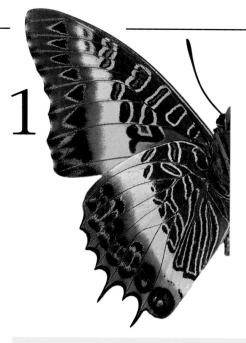

1

2

Sexual reproduction

Simple replication can never give variety, whereas the fossil record shows that many plants and animals have changed rapidly.

Variety occurs when new life is produced from two parents of different sex (see page 20).

Variety is essential if living things are to have the best chance of adapting to any change that may be occurring in the world around.

Charaxes brutus

Similar and different

Look at the two butterflies above. They belong to a species called *Charaxes brutus*. At first glance they look identical, but are they? Make a tracing of each one and put the tracings together. How many differences can you find?

(Butterflies, beetles and other insects are very useful when studying variety because differences between them show up especially well in the pattern of their colour markings. There are many more examples at the end of this book.)

Eudicella gralli

These pictures are of male beetle species called *Eudicella gralli*. The males use the horn on the front of their heads to fight one another for the right to **mate** with a female. Each of the individuals shown along the bottom of this page has a uniquely-shaped horn: a fine example of the variety produced by sexual reproduction (see page 20).

17

How cells copy themselves

Animal and plant cells divide by one of two processes. The simplest process is copying or replication.

Cells in plants and animals are dividing all the time – growth, repair and replacement of tissues all happen by the cells increasing in number. Each new cell must contain all the information it needs to grow to a full sized copy of its 'parent'. In order for this to happen the genes must be copied before the cell divides. This is how it is done.

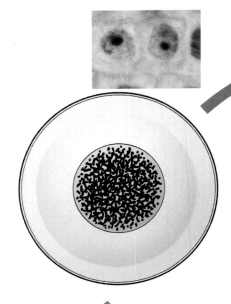

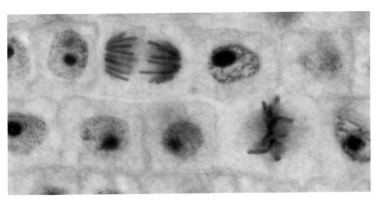

Under the microscope you can see cells dividing in the growing root tip of an onion plant. Different cells are caught at different stages of division and those that are clear have been selected and shown on the relevant place on the diagram to the right.

The time to make new cells

A huge amount of chemical processing has to take place in order to make new cells and yet the whole process takes just a few hours.

This is why, for example, when a person loses blood in an accident, a healthy body can make enough new blood to replace the loss. Blood transfusions are only needed when the loss of blood is very severe.

6 The new fully-grown cell is ready to divide again. In some cases this may be only a matter of minutes away. While in this resting state the chromosomes are thread-like but are too thin to be seen under a microscope.

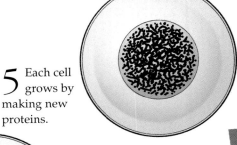

5 Each cell grows by making new proteins.

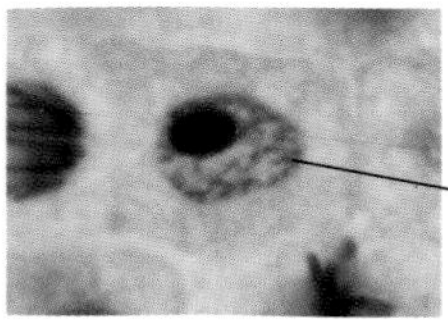

Chromosomes
as long threads
inside the nucleus.

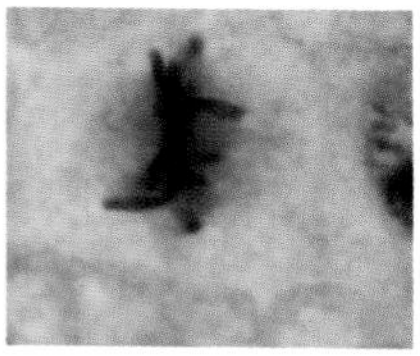

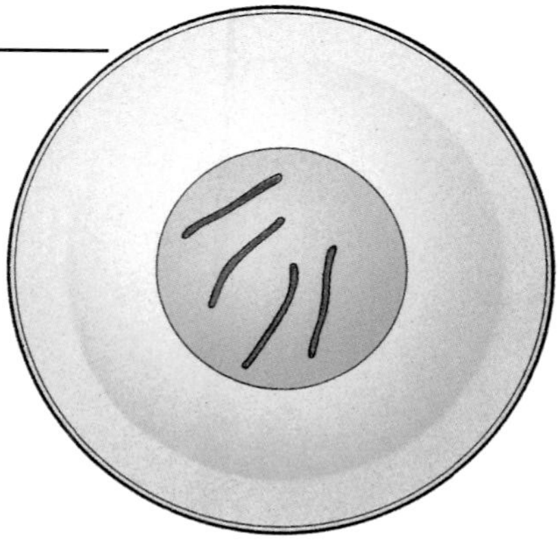

1 The cell prepares for replicating itself. The chromosomes contract and become visible. They start to replicate themselves and each chromosome produces a second identical half. Meanwhile, the membrane around the nucleus dissolves, allowing the chromosomes to move freely inside the whole cell.

2 The chromosomes now become even more visible and can be seen as two halves joined at the middle. Tiny string-like threads appear and make a 'spindle' across the cell. The chromosomes line up on the spindle in the middle of the cell.

Scientists call the process of replication mitosis. The way it works is shown in the diagrams on these pages.

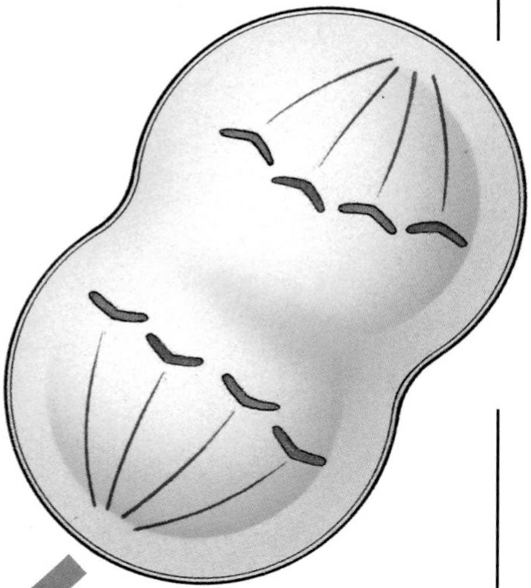

3 Each chromosome splits in half and the halves move to opposite ends of the spindle. Then the cell starts to narrow in the middle.

4 The cell pinches off to make two identical new cells. Each new cell contains exactly the same chromosomes, and therefore genes (genetic code), as the parent cell.

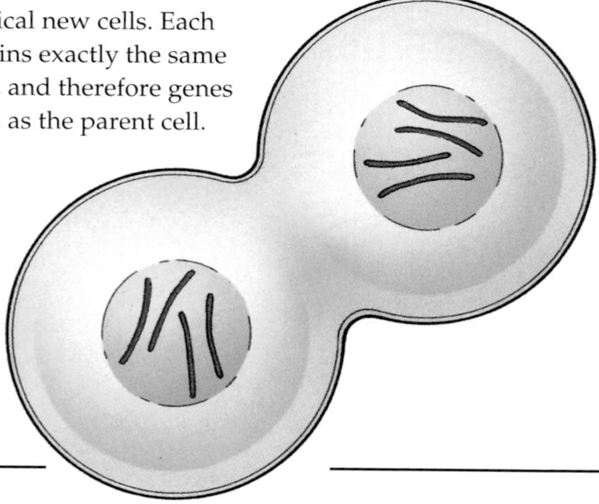

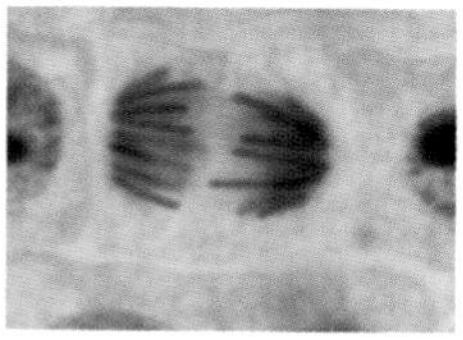

Sex cells

Special sex cells provide the means of creating variety in the members of a species.

These special cells may take weeks to form (in contrast to simple copying which takes just a few hours) because a much more complicated process is involved. When they have been formed sexual reproduction can take place.

These are the female sex cells.

Parent cell divides to produce sex cells

This is a 'parent' cell from a female. It contains a complete set of chromosomes.

Only four chromosomes (two chromosome pairs) are shown to make the diagrams easier to follow.

The formation of sex cells
When sex cells are formed only half of the chromosomes (genetic code) are passed on, or inherited, from the parent cell. For example human sex cells contain only 23 chromosomes whereas the parent cells each contain 46. This half set is not enough to allow the cell to copy itself in the way seen on the previous pages.

Scientists call the process of producing sex cells meiosis (my-o-sis). The way it works is shown in the diagrams on these pages.

Parent cell divides to produce sex cells

This is a 'parent' cell from a male. It contains a complete set of chromosomes.

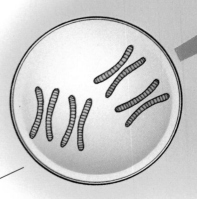

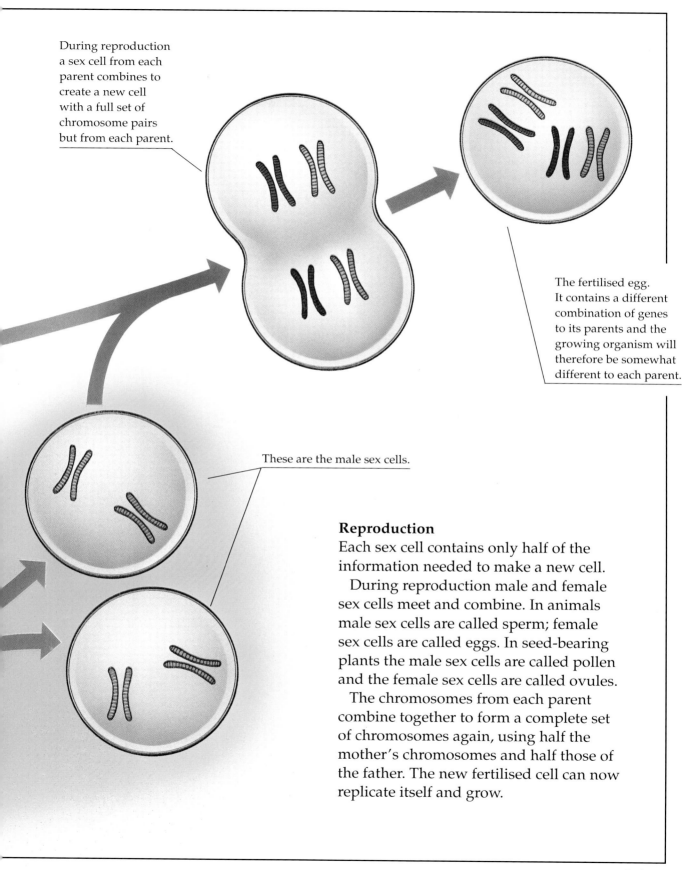

During reproduction a sex cell from each parent combines to create a new cell with a full set of chromosome pairs but from each parent.

The fertilised egg. It contains a different combination of genes to its parents and the growing organism will therefore be somewhat different to each parent.

These are the male sex cells.

Reproduction

Each sex cell contains only half of the information needed to make a new cell.

During reproduction male and female sex cells meet and combine. In animals male sex cells are called sperm; female sex cells are called eggs. In seed-bearing plants the male sex cells are called pollen and the female sex cells are called ovules.

The chromosomes from each parent combine together to form a complete set of chromosomes again, using half the mother's chromosomes and half those of the father. The new fertilised cell can now replicate itself and grow.

Fertilisation

For fertilisation to take place, there has to be a mechanism for the male sex cells to reach the female sex cells. In many plants the male sex cells (pollen) are carried by the wind or animals to the female sex cells in a neighbouring plant.

Sperm can swim easily in water and so, for example, in many cases female fish lay their eggs and the male fish simply releases sperm near to them. Land-based animals, on the other hand, have to unite to provide a way for the sperm to reach the eggs.

1 The sperm cells try to burrow into the egg cell.

Sperm cell with tail

Nucleus of egg cell

Egg cell

Head (containing the nucleus) of the successful sperm cell.

5 After a certain number of divisions (about 16 in humans) the developing egg begins to grow. As more and more cells form, so information from the genes begins to tell each cell how to develop (see page 26).

These diagrams show the fertilisation and initial growth of an egg.

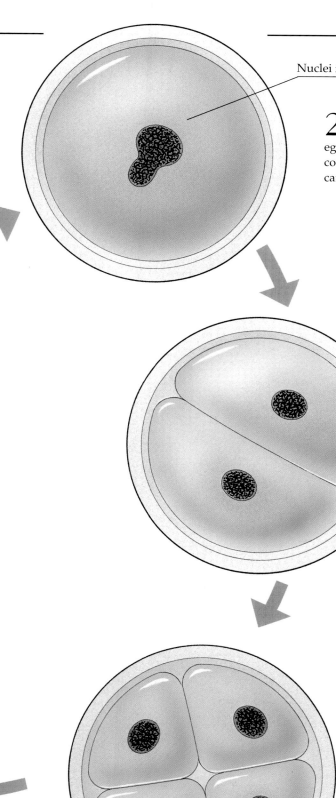

Nuclei fuse

2 Fertilisation. The nucleus of the sperm cell and the nucleus of the egg cell fuse and the chromosomes combine to form a full set. The cell can now copy itself.

3 The cell first divides into two smaller cells and then each of these divides, forming a total of four cells. Further division gives eight cells, then sixteen, thirty two and so on.

Sperm and egg
In animals the sperm has to travel to the egg and it is easier if it is carrying relatively little 'baggage'. So it is a 'slimmed down' version, mainly containing just chromosome parts. It grows a tail to help it swim.

The female egg does not travel and so it retains most of the original cell material and is larger, containing not just chromosome, but proteins and other essential materials for making new cells.

4 To start with, copying simply involves division within the original membrane and the fertilised egg does not grow.

23

A new human life begins

As cells multiply they need to get both a source of nourishment and vital messages about how to grow. On this and the following pages you can follow the story of a fertilised human egg during the immensely complicated process that finally produces a baby.

This is the edge of the womb. It contains strong chemical messages.

1 The fertilised egg attaches itself to the inside part of the mother called the womb. Through the lining of the womb the egg cells get nourished, but it also needs vital chemical messages on how to grow.

Chemical strength

Weak

At this stage the egg is this big.

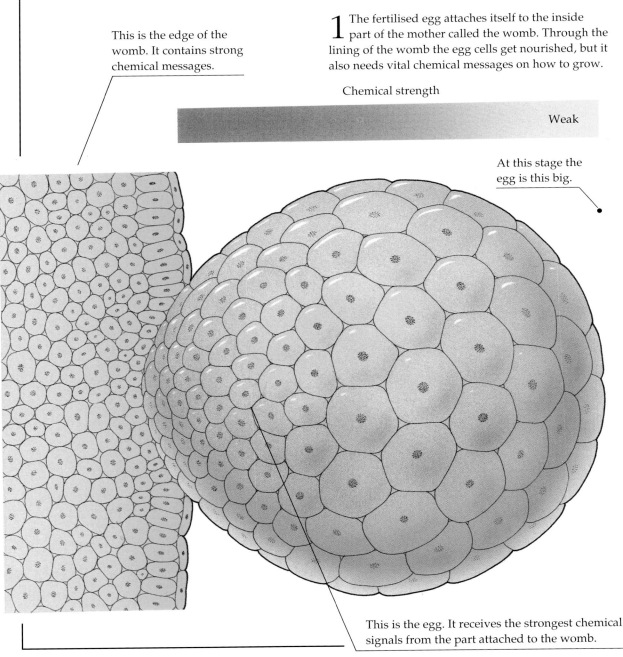

This is the egg. It receives the strongest chemical signals from the part attached to the womb.

2 Chemical messages are sent from the womb lining. These reach every cell in the egg. Where the egg sticks to the womb the chemical messages are strong and this triggers the genes that will make the head; away from the womb the chemical messages are weak and this triggers cells to make the feet.

3 By the strength of the chemical message each cell in the egg knows which 'page' of the genetic recipe book (which group of genes) to switch on and from this it is told how to develop into organs, blood, skin, bone or muscle.

This will become the spine carrying all the messages from the brain to the other parts of the body.

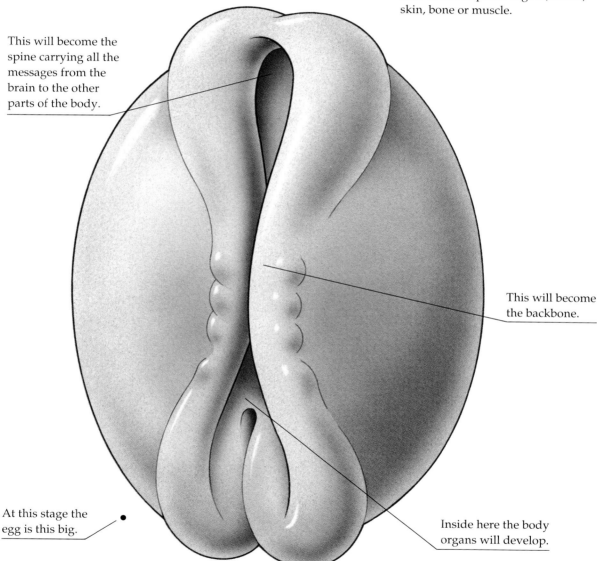

This will become the backbone.

At this stage the egg is this big.

Inside here the body organs will develop.

4 The growing baby is called an **embryo**. The ball of cells begins to fold over on itself, a little bit like dough being folded over when making bread. The fold makes a central tube which, in time, will be the heart, lungs, stomach and other inside parts the body. At one end the head will develop, at the other end will be the feet.

The fetus grows

At the earliest stages of life it is very difficult to tell the embryo of one species from another. But as cells become instructed to specialise in various ways, so each species develops cells that are special to itself. The embryo takes on a much more recognisable shape and is called a fetus.

In a human, what begins as a tiny shapeless ball folds over, stretches, uncurls and grows limbs. During this process genes instruct cells how to give the characteristics that will provide for life outside the womb.

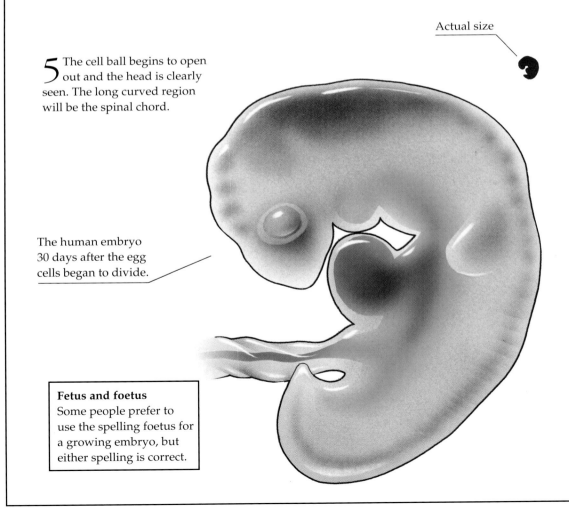

Actual size

5 The cell ball begins to open out and the head is clearly seen. The long curved region will be the spinal chord.

The human embryo 30 days after the egg cells began to divide.

Fetus and foetus
Some people prefer to use the spelling foetus for a growing embryo, but either spelling is correct.

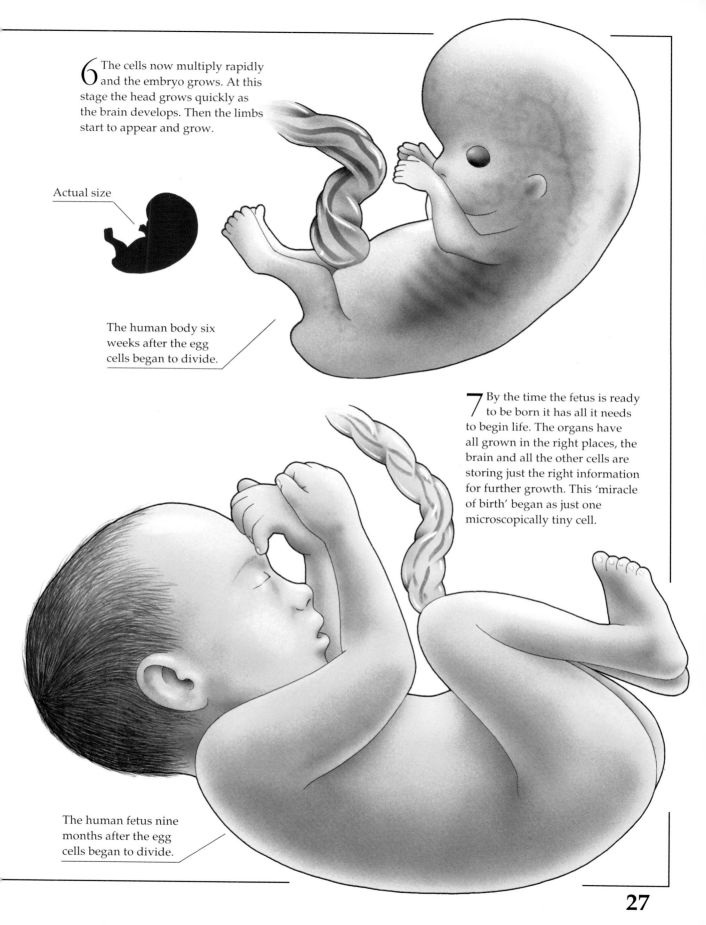

6 The cells now multiply rapidly and the embryo grows. At this stage the head grows quickly as the brain develops. Then the limbs start to appear and grow.

Actual size

The human body six weeks after the egg cells began to divide.

7 By the time the fetus is ready to be born it has all it needs to begin life. The organs have all grown in the right places, the brain and all the other cells are storing just the right information for further growth. This 'miracle of birth' began as just one microscopically tiny cell.

The human fetus nine months after the egg cells began to divide.

Cells specialise

By the time the embryo has developed into a recognisable being, the cells will already have begun to develop along specialised paths. Here are two examples of cells that help to show that the genetic code inside each nucleus is programming its cell to develop for a specific task.

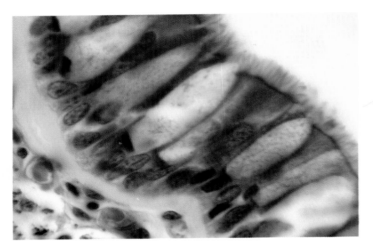

Cleaning cells

Leading from the throat to the lungs is a tube called the windpipe. It is lined with cells which have hair-like protrusions called cilia. Their job is to act as a kind of brush, beating rhythmically in such a way as to sweep back up the throat dirt and other harmful particles that would otherwise reach the delicate lining of the lungs.

(You will find other examples of specialised cells on page 11.)

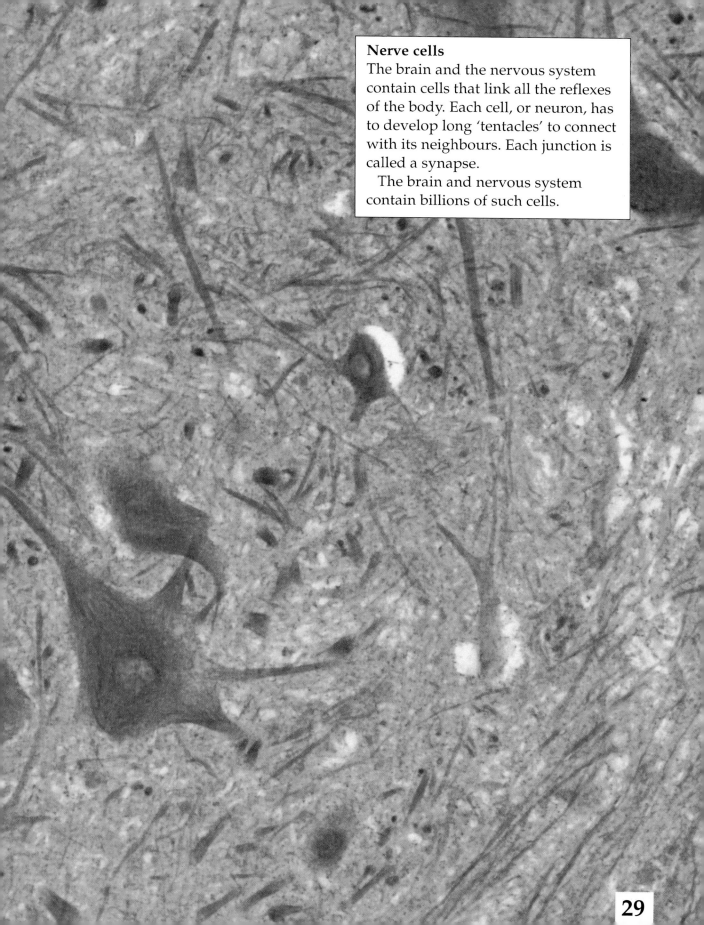

Viruses

Our world contains both large and small organisms, each one of which wants to carry on its line. Humans are among the larger organisms but they are hosts to some of the most tiniest. These, 'microbes', such as viruses, bacteria and amoebas, can reproduce inside our bodies and affect our lives.

On this page you will see how a virus survives. Even though it is far smaller than any of the cells in our bodies, it is very adaptable and quite able to cause us great harm.

1 Virus punctures the skin of a cell.

What is a virus?
A virus is a microscopic parcel of genes bundled inside a ball of fats and proteins. A virus carries a complete set of genes, but it does not have all the ingredients to make a copy of itself. This means that, like all other **parasites**, it has to find a host cell that can be used to help continue the virus line.

Viruses and heredity
A virus is not very good at making accurate copies of its genes. This means that it is continually changing its genetic code.

This means that there will be new varieties all the time. This makes viruses (such as HIV) so difficult to control.

Find out about viruses
Viruses need to be carried from one host to another, and so by causing the host to cough and sneeze they can be spread through the air. This is the fact behind the old saying 'Coughs and sneezes spread diseases'.

Some viruses have caused millions of deaths. The old nursery rhyme 'Ring-a-ring-o'-roses, a pocketful of posies, a-tishoo, a-tishoo, we all fall down!' is believed to have described the European virus plague called the Black Death of the 1600s. See if you can find out about other important viruses, such as influenza, poliomyelitis, smallpox, chickenpox and HIV (the virus linked with AIDS), and see what effects they had or still have.

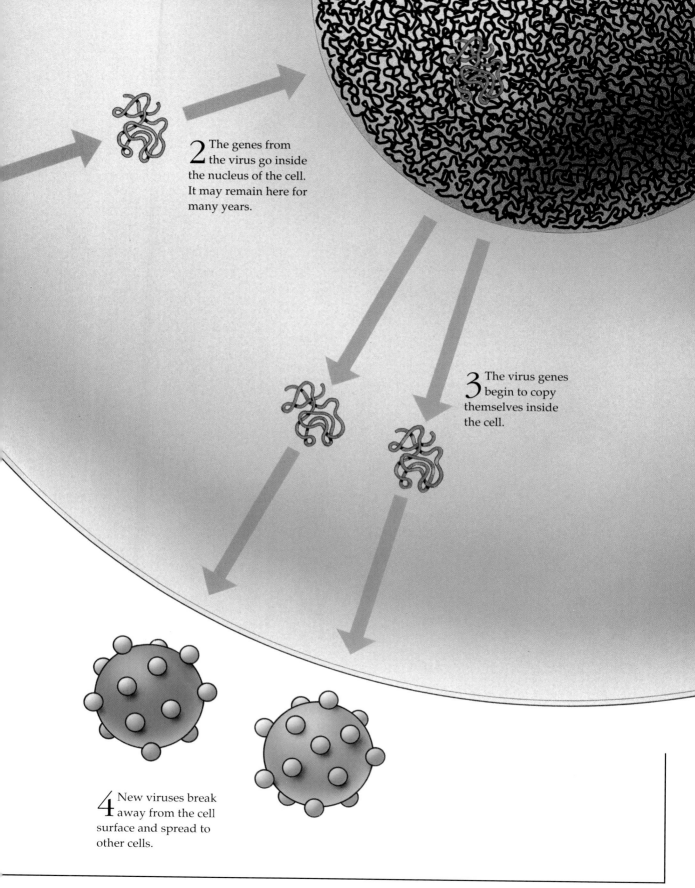

2 The genes from the virus go inside the nucleus of the cell. It may remain here for many years.

3 The virus genes begin to copy themselves inside the cell.

4 New viruses break away from the cell surface and spread to other cells.

How plant breeding works

Pollen, which is the bright yellow dusty substance inside a flower, is the male sex cell. To fertilise a female sex cell at the base of the flower, pollen has to arrive on the stigma and pass down the style to the ovaries. Here is how it happens naturally, and how breeders make use of it for artificial selection.

> **How genes were discovered**
> Gregor Mendel, an Austrian monk who lived during the nineteenth century, discovered the way genes are passed from one generation to another. He experimented by cross-breeding pea plants.

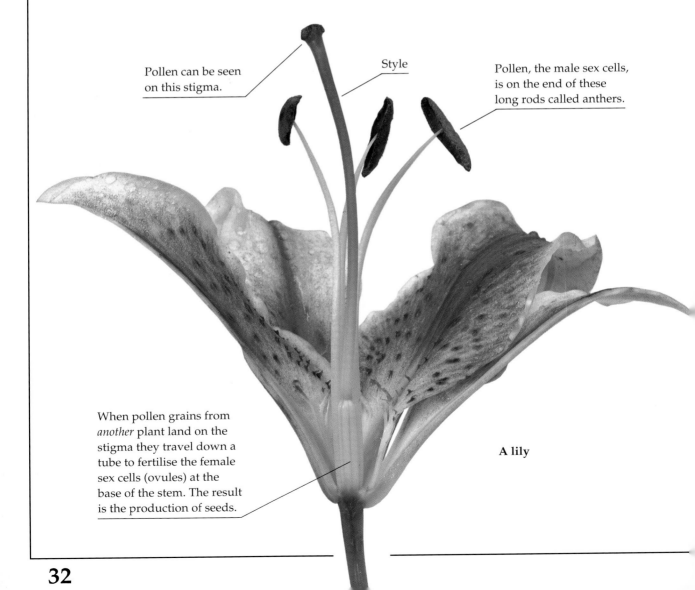

Pollen can be seen on this stigma.

Style

Pollen, the male sex cells, is on the end of these long rods called anthers.

When pollen grains from *another* plant land on the stigma they travel down a tube to fertilise the female sex cells (ovules) at the base of the stem. The result is the production of seeds.

A lily

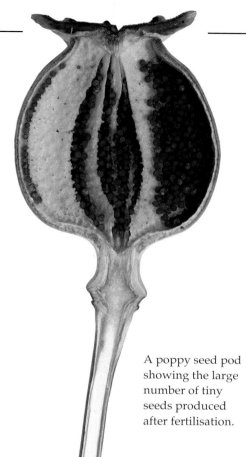

Natural fertilisation

There are three ways this can happen. The wind can easily blow pollen about and some will land on the stigma of another plant of the same species.

Insects, birds and other small animals can carry pollen between plants as they dip into each flower-head in search of nectar.

In some cases the anthers burst and scatter pollen all over the nearby stigma. However, most plants have evolved to prevent such self-fertilisation because the anthers develop at different times to the ovules.

A poppy seed pod showing the large number of tiny seeds produced after fertilisation.

Find out about plant breeding

Follow these steps to see how a plant breeder works to combine the characteristics of two closely related types of potted plant, say potted lilies.

First cut off the anthers from the flowers of one type of plant before they have the chance to scatter their pollen. Then collect pollen from the other type of plant using a fine brush. Brush the pollen on to the stigmas of plants without anthers.

You will soon discover that it is very delicate work.

Hybrids

Hybrid is the general term to describe a cross-breed: the offspring of parents that are distantly related and which would not naturally breed.

Hybrids are produced when people want to get the benefits of special characteristics of the two parents. Here are some examples.

Bigger and better

Hybrids are often bigger and better than their parents. For example, a plant with a sweet smell may be crossed with one having a large flower-head. The hybrid plant may have a large sweet-smelling flower and it may also grow faster and stand up to drought or cold weather better than its parents.

Plant hybrids

Some plants are cross-bred by taking the pollen from one plant and using it to fertilise another. Hybrid corn and wheat have been produced this way (see page 36), but this method has been most often used to produce a wide variety of garden plants.

Animal hybrids

The best known animal hybrid is a mule, which is stronger than either of its parents: a horse and a donkey.

Carnations are a typical example of the use of cross-breeding. They have been bred to match the demands of the buying public.

Investigate hybrids

Look in a seed catalogue or visit a garden shop to find out how many seeds are hybrids. By comparing the hybrid plant description with related plants that are not hybrids can you see which characteristics have been improved?

Notice that the hybrids are usually very much more expensive than 'naturally' fertilised seed because hybrids have to be pollinated by hand.

More uniform

Hybrids tend to produce plants that show far less variety than their parents. Hybrid tomatoes, for example, have been produced so that they are even in size, shape and colour.

Problems with hybrids

Hybrids may not produce any seed at all, or their seed may not breed true and must be discarded. New seed may be produced from further cross-breeding of the parent plants.

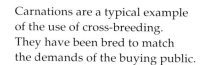

35

Breeding crops for food

Although there are thousands of plant species in the world, you will probably find only about a hundred or so sold in shops. This is because, over the centuries, people have selected out only the plants that are good to eat.

The process that has turned wild species into cultivated crops is another example of plant breeding. Like the flower production shown on page 34, food plant breeding uses methods to alter the natural heredity process for the benefit of people. Here are some important examples.

Wheat

Natural grasses from which wheat has been bred do not look very much like the wheat you can see ripening in the fields. The earliest wheat had completely enclosed grains.

Over the years farmers selected out plants with exposed grains and they bred with these seeds time and time again. By 500 BC 'naked' wheat grains were already common.

Today wheat varieties have far higher yields than in the past, they have shorter, stronger stems so that the plants will not fall over after rain, and they grow to a uniform height to make it easier for machines to harvest.

Rice

Rice is a variety of grass that grows where there is plentiful water. Over seven thousand varieties grow in the wild, but only a few are used for food.

Rice is the most commonly used food grain in the world, partly because it produces one of the highest grain yields.

There have been many attempts to improve the yield of rice, not least because it is the **staple** food of many developing countries. Since the 1960s several high-yielding rice hybrids have been developed and made available to poor farmers, transforming the amount of rice that could be produced in developing countries. This dramatic change in yield was called the **Green Revolution**.

A farmer plants out rice seedlings in Bali, Indonesia.

Corn

Corn or maize is a form of grass, just like wheat and rice. It has been so altered by breeding over past centuries that today the plants would find it difficult to survive in the wild because the ears have been made so large and seed-bearing that they can no longer disperse their seeds themselves. No wild form of maize exists in the world today.

Pepper

The garden vegetable pepper produces not only the green, yellow and red lantern-shaped fruits used in cooking. They also produce the hot chilli, paprika and cayenne peppers used as spices. There are several hundred varieties as well as closely related species including the tomato and the potato. All have been subject to continuous selective breeding.

Gene factories

Because genes are the key to heredity, if the desirable parts of a gene from one cell can be **implanted** into a living cell of another species, then that cell will also carry the new special character when it divides.

This new science is called genetic engineering. In a few years it will be one of the most important branches of science. Here are some examples of its possible effects.

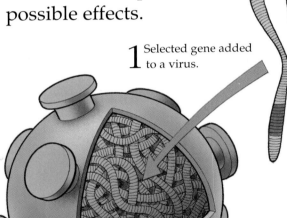

1 Selected gene added to a virus.

2 The gene is incorporated in the virus.

Viruses can bring cures
Some diseases (such as cystic fibrosis) are caused by defective genes. Patients suffering from such diseases can only be cured if the defective genes can be replaced by healthy genes.

Because viruses have a unique ability to burrow into a cell and mix their genes (see page 30) they can be used to repair cells. Scientists are now experimenting by first chemically 'switching' off the virus so that it will not cause illness. Copies of the required gene are added to the DNA of a virus. The virus is then allowed to burrow into and mix with the DNA in human cells that have been taken from the patient. The repaired cells are then returned to the patient.

The green-gene revolution

Scientists are concentrating on altering the genes in plants to be able to improve the shelf-life of fresh food.

For example, food rots because a single gene triggers the production of a special rotting chemical (an enzyme, see page 10). If the genes of plants can be altered so that this trigger gene is switched off, then plants will not rot, neither will they have to be frozen or refrigerated. One way of switching the gene off is by adding a copy of the rotting gene that works in reverse.

If changes of this kind prove successful, they could be of greatest benefit to people in the developing world who do not have access to refrigerators.

Think about gene swaps

Gene swaps will be easy to do in future years and scientists will be able to make many crosses between animals and plants.

As a group discuss some of the benefits and problems that this might cause.

Digesting oil

A bacterium has been altered by changing its DNA so that it digests oil. This means that oil-spills of the future may be digested by bacteria instead of having to be cleaned up using harmful detergents.

How bacteria are changed

Bacteria are small single-celled organisms. They are very promising candidates for genetic engineering because they do not have their DNA bound inside the nucleus. Instead, they have loops of DNA floating around inside the cell. This makes the DNA very much easier to cut open and to implant genes from another species.

As the bacteria divide time after time they automatically produce large amounts of the implanted gene. So, for example, human insulin (needed by people with diabetes) can be produced in large amounts with the help of bacteria, the insulin separated out, and then given to diabetics to help save lives.

3 The virus enters the body cells.

4 The healthy gene is added to the body cells.

Natural selection

Natural selection is a theory put forward by Charles Darwin. He suggested that the variation we see between species can be explained by the natural changes that take place from one generation to the next.

Find similar groups
Look at the beetles on this page and lay a sheet of tracing paper over them.
   Try to find ones which might be related, and mark each group with a differently coloured pen or with a number on the tracing paper. Then check your selections with the answers on page 47.

What Darwin thought

In 1859 Charles Darwin wrote a book called the *Origin of Species*. He looked at the natural variation that exists within and between species. Darwin suggested some natural reasons for this variation. For example, any inherited character that made it easier to hide from a enemy would be more likely to be passed on from generation to generation because those which could hide well would be more likely to survive. This process is known as natural selection by the 'survival of the fittest'.

In real life there are many successful ways of staying alive, and therefore many successful adaptations can be passed through the generations. In time, Darwin argued, these naturally selected adaptations would allow the development of separate species, accounting for the great variety of life we see today.

What fossils show

A fossil is the preserved remains of a plant or animal that was alive a long time ago. Many fossil remains are found in rocks and they are hundreds of millions of years old. This gives a great opportunity to investigate how natural changes have taken place through geological time.

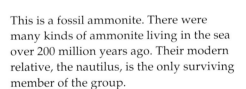

This is a fossilised example of a fly. Millions of years ago this fly was buried in the sap from a tree. The sap was later buried and made into rock-like material called amber. This perfectly-preserved specimen looks quite like its modern relatives.

This is a fossil ammonite. There were many kinds of ammonite living in the sea over 200 million years ago. Their modern relative, the nautilus, is the only surviving member of the group.

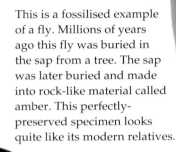

Darwin and the geological record

The fossil record in the rocks gives a good indication of what has happened through millions of years of history.

Such a long period of time should have given many opportunities for the character of species to change markedly from their ancestors.

In practice the fossil record shows examples of both those that have not changed much (on this page) and those that show great variation (opposite).

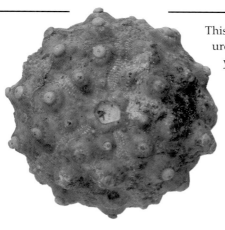

This is the fossil remains of a sea urchin from about 160 million years ago (it is called *Cideris*). It originally had long spines that were used to lodge itself among rocks near the shore, just as some sea urchins do today.

This fossil sea urchin is called *Hemicideris*. It is clearly different in pattern from the *Cideris*, although it lived at the same time.

This is the fossil remains of a sea urchin called *Micraster*. It lived about 100 million years ago, but it did not have long spines because it burrowed in the sand. Notice that its body shape is also different from the *Cideris*. *Micraster* may have adapted its shape from the older sea urchins.

This is the shell of a present-day sea urchin. It has a much smoother surface than its ancient relatives, although in life it still has long spines.

This is the shell of a present-day sand dollar. It is also a sea urchin, but it is flattened so that it can live on sandy sea beds. It has a smooth surface like *Micraster*.

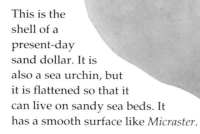

Camouflage and mimicry

It is quite common to find two unrelated species with some similar characteristic such as colour or pattern. It is also common to find animals that have colours similar to their surroundings. In both cases the genes for colour have produced a survival advantage.

This is a stick insect. Its body has a colour, shape and texture that make it seem like the twigs of its surroundings. It can also remain still for long periods, hiding from enemies.

This is a green lizard. Its colour closely resembles that of the leaves near its home.

A lizard must bask in the sunshine to warm up, but this makes it vulnerable to enemies. Its camouflage pattern makes it difficult to spot and thus increases its chance of survival.

Mimicry and camouflage

The word mimicry comes from the Greek *mimos*, 'imitator'. Biologists use the word mimicry to describe the way some creatures resemble each other, perhaps in colour, pattern or shape. They do not mean that one species intended to copy, or imitate the other.

In a similar way biologists use the word 'camouflage' to describe the way that some species are not easily seen in their surroundings. Biologists do not mean to suggest that the creatures intended to develop this kind of pattern.

Model
Danaus crysippus
Poisonous to birds

Mimic
Hypolimnas missippus
Edible to birds

Model
Amauris albimaculata
Poisonous to birds

Mimic
Hypolimnas deceptor
Edible to birds

Mimic butterflies

Some butterflies are poisonous to eat and they will be avoided by birds. Other butterflies are not poisonous, but they have similar markings, so birds tend to leave them alone as well.

This accidental mimicking of colour and pattern serves the 'mimic' well, and the genes for colour and pattern have given a survival advantage.

New words

blueprint
in engineering a blueprint is an original plan or model that plays a major role in influencing the design of the finished product. Biologists borrowed the name to make it easier for people to visualise the role of the gene pattern in life

cell
the simplest form of independent life. At its centre is a nucleus which contains the genes which act as the blueprint for future generations. Surrounding the nucleus are the parts that provide it with nourishment and energy

colonise
to become established in a new area. In places where there is severe competition, the most successful colonist is often the plant that can reproduce fastest

DNA
Deoxyribonucleic acid (DNA) and ribonucleic acid (RNA) are the two chemical substances used to transfer information about heredity from parent to offspring. They are called nucleic acids because they are found in the core, or nucleus, of each cell

embryo
an animal in the early stages of development after the fertilised cell has begun to divide. After 8 weeks development a human embryo is called a fetus

fertilised egg
a female sex cell that has been united with a male sex cell to make an egg that can grow into a new plant or animal

fossil
the remains of a plant or animal that is found in rocks. It may consist of a cast, a mould or as altered tissue and bone

gene
the strings of coded chemical packets that provide a blueprint for life

Green Revolution
the introduction of special high-yielding varieties of crops and modern farming methods to developing countries

implant
to attach firmly

inherit
to gain a characteristic passed on through the genes

mammals
mammals are a group of animals that give birth to live young and are fed by their mother's milk

mate
to reproduce sexually

molecule
the smallest possible particle of a substance. Everything around us, including ourselves, is made of molecules

This illustration shows groups of beetles that are closely related. See page 41 for the complete activity.

1 = Goliath beetles, flower beetles and sapchafers   **2** = True scarab beetles   **3** = Stag beetles
4 = Hercules and rhinoceros beetles   **5** = Long-armed beetles   **6** = Cockchafers
7 = Shining leafchafers   **8** = Long-horned beetles   **9** = Jewel beetles
10 = Spider-hunting wasps (not beetles)   **11** = Click beetles   **12** = Ground beetles

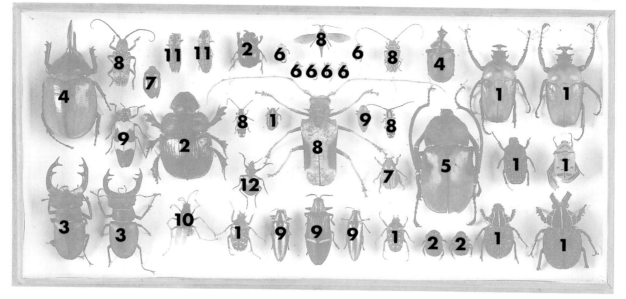

niche
a particularly suitable position amongst all the other living things in a locality

parasite
an animal or plant that lives within or on another – called the host – and from which it receives essential nourishment. The host does not benefit from the presence of a parasite and is often harmed by it

protein
a substance that acts as the main building-block of all tissue

reproduction
one of two ways that an animal or plant produces new life similar to itself

species
a group of plants or animals that can breed among its members. Oaks make up a species because pollen from one oak can fertilise a flower from another oak

staple
a staple crop is one that is used to provide most of the food for a community. Wheat, maize, and rice are all examples of staple crops

trait
a characteristic feature of a plant or animal which helps to distinguish it from others of the same species

Index